Learn La

Practical Guide

A. De Quattro

Guide to Laravel

1.Introduction to Laravel

Laravel is an open-source PHP framework created by Taylor Otwell in 2011, which has gained great popularity among developers for its ease of use, versatility, and robustness. Thanks to its clear and intuitive syntax, Laravel allows for the rapid and efficient development of complex and high-quality web applications.

The framework is based on the MVC (Model-View-Controller) architectural pattern, which promotes the separation of business logic, presentation, and data management. This allows for more organized and maintainable code, making teamwork easier and enabling developers to focus more on the application's logic.

One of Laravel's strengths is its wide range of built-in features, also known as "services," which significantly simplify application development. Some examples of services included in Laravel are Authentication, Authorization, Routing, Caching, Events, and Unit Testing. These services help developers save time and effort by providing ready-to-use functionality.

Laravel also offers a packaging system called "Laravel packages," which allows developers to easily add additional features to their applications. This system enables the integration of external libraries, third-party packages, and custom components without having to write code from scratch.

Another important feature of Laravel is the Eloquent ORM (Object-Relational Mapping), which greatly simplifies data and relationship management within the application. This system allows for easily defining models for database tables and interacting with them using intuitive methods and queries.

Laravel also features a powerful template system called "Blade," which allows for the easy creation of responsive and dynamic layouts for web pages. The Blade templating system enables the inclusion of PHP code blocks directly in HTML files without compromising code readability.

The framework also provides a robust error and exception handling system that allows developers to easily find and resolve any issues in the application. Laravel also offers an event logging system that allows for monitoring and analyzing application activity in real-time.

Lastly, Laravel includes a set of tools for automated application testing, which enable the verification of code correctness and functionality. With these tools, developers can write unit tests, integration tests, and functional tests to ensure the quality and stability of the application.

Laravel is a powerful, flexible, and reliable framework that provides developers with all the necessary tools to efficiently and professionally develop modern and high-performing web applications. Its growing popularity and active community support make it an ideal choice for anyone looking to create successful web applications.

2. Installation of Laravel

To install Laravel, the recommended method is through the use of Composer, a PHP dependency manager.

Here is a detailed guide on how to install Laravel using Composer:

1. To get started, make sure you have Composer installed on your computer. If you don't already have it, you can download and install it from the official Composer website.

2. Open the terminal on your computer and navigate your working directory to the folder where you want to install Laravel.

3. Once in the correct folder, run the following command to create a new Laravel project:

```
```

composer create-project --prefer-dist
laravel/laravel project-name

```
```

Replace "project-name" with the name you
want to give to your Laravel project.

4. Composer will start downloading and
installing all the necessary files for your
Laravel project. This may take a few minutes
depending on the speed of your internet
connection.

5. Once the installation is complete, navigate
to your Laravel project directory and run the
following command to start the Laravel
integrated development server:

```
```

php artisan serve

```
```

This command will start a local server and provide you with a URL to access your Laravel application through the browser.

6. Now you can start developing your Laravel application! You can modify the files in the "app" directory to write the PHP code for your application, and refer to the official Laravel documentation for more information on how to use the framework.

By following these steps, you should be able to successfully install Laravel using Composer and start developing your web application in PHP.

3. The Model-View-Controller (MVC) architecture

The Model-View-Controller (MVC) architecture of Laravel is one of the most powerful and significant features of this PHP framework. This architectural pattern divides the application into three distinct layers: the model, the view, and the controller, each with a specific task.

The model represents the application data and handles the business logic. It includes the logic for accessing and manipulating data in the database, such as queries to retrieve, update, create, or delete records. Models in Laravel are represented by Eloquent classes, which make interacting with the database using an Object-Oriented interface easier.

The view handles the presentation of data to the end user. In Laravel, views are Blade files, which allow for clean and readable mixing of

HTML and PHP. This enables separating the presentation logic from the business logic, making code maintenance and management easier.

The controller acts as an intermediary between the model and the view. It handles user requests, queries the model to retrieve the necessary data, and passes it to the view for presentation. Controllers in Laravel are classes that define methods to handle various application actions, such as displaying a page, creating a new record, or updating an existing record.

Laravel makes implementing the MVC architecture easier by providing tools and specific functionalities to manage different aspects of the application. For example, routing allows handling HTTP requests and routing them to the corresponding controllers, while Eloquent simplifies interacting with the database using an intuitive API based on Object-Relational Mapping (ORM).

The Model-View-Controller (MVC) architecture of Laravel is one of the main reasons why the framework is so popular among web developers. This structure enables a clear separation between business logic, data presentation, and user interactions management, making the code cleaner, organized, and maintainable.

In the following examples, we will illustrate how the MVC architecture of Laravel works using a simple task management system.

1. Model

The model represents the data of our system and contains the business logic. Let's create a Task model that represents a task to be completed:

```php
namespace App\Models;
```

```
use Illuminate\Database\Eloquent\Model;


class Task extends Model
{
    protected $fillable = ['title', 'description', 'status'];
}
```

2. View

The view is responsible for presenting data to users. Let's create a blade view that displays a list of tasks:

```html
<!-- tasks.blade.php -->
@foreach($tasks as $task)
```

```
<div>

  <h3>{{ $task->title }}</h3>

  <p>{{ $task->description }}</p>

</div>

@endforeach

```
```

3. Controller

The controller acts as an intermediary between the model and the view, handling user requests and returning appropriate responses. Let's create a TaskController that will handle CRUD operations on tasks:

```php
namespace App\Http\Controllers;


use Illuminate\Http\Request;

use App\Models\Task;
```
```

```php
class TaskController extends Controller
{
  public function index()
  {
    $tasks = Task::all();
    return view('tasks', compact('tasks'));
  }

  public function store(Request $request)
  {
    Task::create($request->all());
    return redirect()->route('tasks.index');
  }

  public function update(Request $request, Task $task)
  {
```

```
    $task->update($request->all());

    return redirect()->route('tasks.index');

  }


  public function destroy(Task $task)

  {

    $task->delete();

    return redirect()->route('tasks.index');

  }

}
```

These are just a few examples of how the MVC architecture of Laravel is structured. Of course, it is possible to customize and extend this structure based on the specific needs of the project. Laravel offers many tools and features that make web development more efficient and enjoyable.

4. Routing in Laravel

Laravel offers a very powerful and flexible routing system that allows to effectively handle HTTP requests within a web application.

To define routes in Laravel, you can use the file routes/web.php located in the routes folder of the project. In this file, you can define routes using the Route::get, Route::post, Route::put, Route::patch, Route::delete, Route::any, or Route::match methods, depending on the HTTP method you want to handle.

For example, to define a route that responds to a GET request at the "/" URL, you can simply write:

Route::get('/', function () {

```
    return view('welcome');

});
```

In this case, when a user visits the site and requests the homepage, Laravel will return the view with the name "welcome".

You can also define parameterized routes, which allow passing parameters directly in the URL. For example, to define a route that accepts an "id" parameter and returns it in the response, you can write:

```
Route::get('/user/{id}', function ($id) {

    return 'User ' . $id;

});
```

This way, if the user visits the URL /user/1, Laravel will return the string "User 1".

Furthermore, you can group routes to apply certain rules to multiple routes simultaneously, such as using middleware to verify user authentication. To do this, you can use the Route::middleware method:

```
Route::middleware(['auth'])->group(function () {
    Route::get('/dashboard', function () {
        return view('dashboard');
    });
});
```

In this case, the "/dashboard" route will only be accessible to authenticated users, as a middleware that verifies authentication has been applied.

In general, Laravel's routing system is very powerful and offers many advanced features to effectively and flexibly handle HTTP requests. Thanks to its clarity and flexibility, it allows to efficiently manage the various pages and functionalities of a web application.

In Laravel, routing is the mechanism that defines how the application responds to HTTP requests. This means that when a user visits a specific URL, Laravel determines which code to execute to fulfill that request.

Route definition in Laravel can be done in the `routes/web.php` or `routes/api.php` file, depending on the type of route being defined. Routes defined in `routes/web.php` are used for traditional HTTP requests, while routes defined in `routes/api.php` are used for creating APIs.

Let's see some examples of how to define routes in Laravel:

1. Basic route

```php
Route::get('/', function () {
    return view('welcome');
});
```

In this example, we are defining a route that matches the base URL of our site. When a user visits the site's URL, the `welcome` view will be displayed.

2. Route with parameter

```php
Route::get('/user/{id}', function ($id) {
    return 'User ID: '.$id;
});
```

```
```

In this example, we are defining a route that accepts a parameter `{id}` in the URL. When a user visits a URL like `/user/1`, it will return "User ID: 1".

3. Route with Controller

```php

Route::get('/users', 'UserController@index');

```

In this example, we are defining a route that points to the `index` method of the `UserController` controller. When a user visits the URL `/users`, the `index` method of the controller will be called to handle the request.

4. Route with middleware

```php

Route::get('/admin', function () {

    //
```

```
})->middleware('auth');
```

In this example, we are defining a route that is protected by an authentication middleware. This means that only authenticated users can access the `/admin` URL.

5. Creating controllers and models in Laravel Interface with the database using Eloquent ORM

Laravel is a very powerful and flexible PHP framework that allows you to easily build complex web applications. One of the main features of Laravel is the Object-Relational Mapping (ORM) called Eloquent, which greatly facilitates interfacing with the database.

To create controllers and models in Laravel, you just need to use the Artisan commands provided by the framework. For example, to create a new controller, you can use the command:

```php
php artisan make:controller ControllerName
```

This command will create a new PHP file inside the "app/Http/Controllers" folder that can be used to define the actions that the controller should perform.

To create a new model, you can use the command:

```php
php artisan make:model ModelName
```

This command will create a new PHP file inside the "app" folder that will contain the model definition.

Once the controllers and models are defined, you can interface with the database using Eloquent. This ORM allows you to define relationships between database tables through logical relationships within the models.

For example, if you want to define a "one-to-many" relationship between two tables, you can do so inside the model like this:

```php
class User extends Model
{
    public function posts()
    {
        return $this->hasMany(Post::class);
    }
}
```

In this case, the User model has a "one-to-many" relationship with the Post model, so each user can have multiple associated posts.

To interact with the database, you can use the

methods provided by Eloquent such as "find", "create", "where", etc. Example of usage:

```php
$user = User::find(1);

$posts = $user->posts;
```

This query will select the user with ID 1 and retrieve all the posts associated with that user.

In this way, Laravel greatly simplifies interfacing with the database through the use of Eloquent ORM, allowing you to focus on the application logic rather than SQL queries.

6. Creating views and templates in Laravel Using Blade for template management

In Laravel, views and templates are fundamental elements for creating dynamic and personalized web pages. Views represent the web pages that will be displayed to the user, while templates are files that contain the structure and layout of a web page.

To create a new view in Laravel, simply use the command `php artisan make:view view_name`. This command will create a new file inside the `resources/views` folder with the specified name. Inside this file, you can insert the HTML, CSS, and JavaScript code necessary for the page display.

To use a template in Laravel, you can make use of the Blade template engine. Blade is a simple and powerful template engine that allows you to write PHP code within template files in a more readable and intuitive way.

For example, to create a template that includes a common header and footer for all pages of the site, you can create two separate files `header.blade.php` and `footer.blade.php` inside the `resources/views` folder. Then, you can include these files in each view using the `@include('header')` and `@include('footer')` directives.

Additionally, Blade offers many other useful commands such as the ability to use loops, conditions, and variables within templates. For example, you can use the `@foreach` syntax to loop through an array of data and automatically generate HTML code for each element of the array.

In conclusion, creating views and templates in Laravel is essential for creating dynamic and well-structured web pages. By using Blade, you can simplify template management and improve code readability, making the web development process more effective and enjoyable.

In Laravel, views and templates are used to organize and display the content of web pages. To create a view in Laravel, you can use the artisan command `make:view` followed by the desired view name. For example, to create a view called `welcome.blade.php`, you can use the following command:

```bash
php artisan make:view welcome
```

After creating the view, you can use Blade, Laravel's integrated template engine, to manage the layout of the page. Blade offers a simple and powerful syntax to insert variables, conditions, and loops within templates.

Here is an example of how you could use

Blade inside a Laravel view:

```html
<!DOCTYPE html>
<html>
<head>
    <title>Welcome</title>
</head>
<body>
    <h1>{{ $title }}</h1>

    <ul>
        @foreach($items as $item)
            <li>{{ $item }}</li>
        @endforeach
    </ul>

    @if($showMessage)
```

```
    <p>{{ $message }}</p>

  @endif

</body>

</html>

```

In this example, the view `welcome.blade.php` uses variables like `$title`, `$items`, `$showMessage`, and `$message`. These variables can be passed to the view from the controller using the `view()->with()` method. For example:

```php
public function welcome()
{
    $title = 'Welcome to Laravel';

    $items = ['Item 1', 'Item 2', 'Item 3'];

    $showMessage = true;
```

```
    $message = 'This is a welcome message';


    return view('welcome')-
>with(compact('title', 'items', 'showMessage',
'message'));

}
```

This way, the `welcome.blade.php` view will receive the necessary variables to display the content dynamically. This allows for creating flexible and reusable layouts using Blade in Laravel.

7. Passing data to views Creating basic layout for website in Laravel

To pass data to views in Laravel, we can use the `with()` method inside the controller. For example, if we need to pass an array of data to the view `welcome.blade.php`, we can do so like this:

```php
// HomeController.php

public function index()
{
    $data = [
        'title' => 'Welcome to our website',
        'subtitle' => 'Discover amazing products and services'
    ];
```

```
    return view('welcome')->with($data);

}
```

In the `welcome.blade.php` file, we can now access the data passed from the controller using Blade syntax:

```html
<!-- welcome.blade.php -->
<!DOCTYPE html>
<html>
<head>
    <title>{{ $title }}</title>
</head>
<body>
    <h1>{{ $subtitle }}</h1>
```

```
</body>

</html>
```

This way, the controller passes data to the view and the view can access and display it in the website layout.

For creating a basic layout for the website in Laravel, we can use Blade layout files. Let's create a `layout.blade.php` file that will contain the basic structure of our website:

```html
<!-- layout.blade.php -->

<!DOCTYPE html>

<html>

<head>

    <title>@yield('title')</title>
```

```html
    <link rel="stylesheet" href="css/styles.css">
</head>
<body>
    <header>
        <h1>My Website</h1>
    </header>

    <div class="content">
        @yield('content')
    </div>

    <footer>
        <p>&copy; 2022 My Website</p>
    </footer>
</body>
</html>
```

```
```

We can now extend this base layout in our specific views using the `@extends` directive and the `@section` tags:

```html
<!-- welcome.blade.php -->
@extends('layout')

@section('title', 'Welcome')

@section('content')
    <h1>Welcome to our website</h1>
    <p>Discover amazing products and services</p>
@endsection
```

This way, we can have a base layout for our Laravel website and use specific views to add unique content.

8. Request Management in Laravel Using Middleware for Request Management

In Laravel, request management is crucial to ensure that received requests are processed correctly and securely. One of the most common techniques for managing requests in Laravel is using Middleware.

Middleware in Laravel are filters that are executed before or after processing an HTTP request. These filters allow adding additional functionalities to request management, such as data validation, user authorization, session management, and more.

To create a Middleware in Laravel, simply use the artisan command `php artisan make:middleware MiddlewareName`. This command will create a new file in the `app/Http/Middleware` folder containing the code for the newly created Middleware.

Once the Middleware is created, it can be registered in the `$middleware` array in the `app/Http/Kernel.php` file. This way, the Middleware will be executed for every HTTP request received by the application.

There are multiple use cases for Middleware in Laravel. For example, a Middleware can be created to check if the user is authenticated before allowing access to certain application resources. This ensures the security of sensitive information within the application.

Furthermore, Middleware can also be used to validate data sent with an HTTP request. For instance, a Middleware can be created to validate form data before allowing the application to proceed with processing such data.

Ultimately, using Middleware in Laravel is

essential to efficiently and securely manage incoming HTTP requests. Thanks to the flexibility and power of Middleware, multiple advanced functionalities can be implemented to enhance request management and ensure the application's security. In Laravel, Middleware can be used to manage incoming requests before they are passed to the controller. Middleware allows filtering and modifying requests based on certain conditions.

To create a custom Middleware, you can use the command `php artisan make:middleware MiddlewareName`. This command will create a file inside the `app/Http/Middleware` folder, where you can define the logic to be executed before passing the request to the controller.

Here is an example of Middleware that checks if the user is authenticated and, if not, redirects to the login page:

```php
```

```php
<?php

namespace App\Http\Middleware;

use Closure;
use Illuminate\Support\Facades\Auth;

class Authenticate
{
    public function handle($request, Closure $next)
    {
        if (Auth::check()) {
            return $next($request);
        }

        return redirect()->route('login');
```

```
    }

}
```

Per utilizzare il Middleware appena creato, è possibile registrarlo nel file `app/Http/Kernel.php` nel array `$routeMiddleware`:

```php
protected $routeMiddleware = [

    'auth' =>
\App\Http\Middleware\Authenticate::class,

];
```

Finally, you can associate the Middleware to a route in the `routes/web.php` file:

```php
Route::get('/dashboard', function () {
    // This route requires authentication
})->middleware('auth');
```

This way, every request to the `/dashboard` route will pass through the `Authenticate` middleware, which will check if the user is authenticated and redirect them to the login page if necessary.

Middleware can be used for various purposes, such as access control, input data validation, request logging, and much more. They are a powerful tool for request management in Laravel.

9. Creating forms and data validation in Laravel File Upload

Laravel offers many useful features for data management and form creation. In this short guide, I will explain how to create a form and validate the data entered in it using Laravel.

First of all, it is necessary to create a route that points to the controller that will handle our form. For example, we can create a route that points to the "createForm" method of the "FormController":

```php
Route::get('/form',
'FormController@createForm');
```

Next, we define our controller with the "createForm" method that will return the form view:

```php
public function createForm()
{
    return view('form');
}
```

Once the form view is created, we can proceed with the validation of the entered data. Laravel offers convenient functions for data validation. We can use the "validate" method in the controller to validate the data entered in the form:

```php
public function submitForm(Request $request)
```

```
{
    $validatedData = $request->validate([
        'name' => 'required|string',
        'email' => 'required|email',
    ]);
}
```

In this example, we are validating the "name" and "email" fields of the form. The "name" field must be required and of type string, while the "email" field must be required and have a valid email format.

Once the validation is done, we can proceed with submitting the data to the database or perform other necessary operations.

Now let's move on to file uploads with Laravel. To allow users to upload files through the form, we can use the "file" method in the "validate" method of the controller:

```php
$validatedData = $request->validate([
    'name' => 'required|string',
    'email' => 'required|email',
    'file' => 'required|file',
]);
```

This way we are also validating the "file" field, which must be required and of file type. Laravel will automatically handle the file upload and save it in the default storage directory.

To display the uploaded file in the form, we can use the Laravel "file" method in the view:

```html
<form action="/submit" method="post" enctype="multipart/form-data">
    @csrf
    <input type="text" name="name">
    <input type="email" name="email">
    <input type="file" name="file">
    <button type="submit">Submit</button>
</form>
```

In this way, we are allowing users to upload a file along with form data. Once the submit button is clicked, the data will be validated and saved in the database, while the file will be uploaded and saved in the Laravel storage directory. With Laravel, it is very easy to create forms and validate the input data, as well as manage file uploads. The framework offers many useful functions for efficiently and securely handling these operations.

10. Authentication and Authorization in Laravel Implementing an authentication system

Laravel offers a robust and flexible authentication system that allows users to be authenticated based on their credentials.

To implement authentication in Laravel, the first thing to do is to create a table in the database to store user information. Laravel provides an integrated authentication system that makes it easy to manage user authentication. To get started, you can run the command `php artisan make:auth` to automatically generate the views, controllers, and routes needed for authentication.

Once the views, controllers, and routes for authentication are created, you can start using Laravel's authentication system. For example, to authenticate a user, you can use the `attempt` method of Laravel's `Auth` class.

Here's an example of authenticating a user:

```
if (Auth::attempt(['email' => $email,
'password' => $password])) {

    // The user has been successfully
authenticated

    return redirect()->intended('dashboard');

}
```

Once the user is authenticated, you can use Laravel's middleware to protect routes that require authentication. For example, to protect a route, you can use the `auth` middleware in the web routes file:

```
Route::get('/dashboard',
'DashboardController@index')-
```

```
>middleware('auth');
```

Additionally, Laravel offers an authorization system that allows you to define user roles and permissions. For example, you can define a policy to check if a user can modify a certain model. For example:

```
public function update(User $user, Post $post)
{
    return $user->id === $post->user_id;
}
```

This way, you can use Laravel's authorization system to manage user permissions based on their roles and privileges. This is just a brief example of how to implement authentication and authorization in Laravel, but there are many other features and possibilities offered by the framework to securely manage user access to the application's resources.

11. Creation of user permissions and roles Protection of routes with authentication middleware

Creating user permissions and roles is a critical component in managing computer systems to ensure the security and privacy of data. Permissions determine what actions a user can perform within the system, while roles group together a set of permissions to simplify access management.

To create user permissions and roles, it is necessary to first define which actions should be available within the system and assign each a level of authorization. For example, a permission could be "edit post" or "view financial report".

Once permissions are defined, roles can be created that group together different permissions. For example, we could have an "administrator" role that includes permissions such as "edit post" and "delete post", while a "standard user" role might only have the permission to "view post".

To protect routes with authentication middleware, it is necessary to verify that the user attempting to access a route has the necessary permissions to do so. For example, if you want to protect a route that allows for editing a post, you can use middleware to check if the authenticated user has the "edit post" permission before allowing access to the route.

Here is an example of how authentication middleware could be implemented in a web application:

```javascript
const express = require('express');

const app = express();
```

```
app.use((req, res, next) => {

    // Verifica se l'utente è autenticato

    if (!loggedIn) {

        return res.status(401).json({ message:
'Utente non autenticato' });

    }


    // Verifica se l'utente ha il permesso
necessario

    if (!checkPermission(req.user, 'modifica
post')) {

        return res.status(403).json({ message:
'Permesso negato' });

    }


    next();
});
```

```javascript
app.put('/posts/:id', (req, res) => {

    // Modifica il post

    res.json({ message: 'Post modificato con
successo' });

});


function checkPermission(user, permission) {

    // Logica per verificare se l'utente ha il
permesso

    return
user.permissions.includes(permission);

}


const loggedIn = true;

const user = {

    id: 1,

    name: 'Alice',

    permissions: ['modifica post']
```

```
};


app.listen(3000, () => {

    console.log('Server avviato su porta 3000');

});
```
```

In this example, the middleware checks if the user is authenticated and has permission to "edit post" before allowing access to the post edit route. If the user is not authenticated or does not have the necessary permission, a status code of 401 or 403 will be returned respectively.
```

By using permissions and user roles along with authentication middleware, it is possible to ensure that only authorized users can access sensitive resources within the system, helping to improve security and access management.

12. Error handling in Laravel Creating custom error pages

In Laravel, error handling is a very important aspect in order to provide users with an optimal user experience.

To handle errors in Laravel, you can use the `App\Exceptions\Handler` middleware, which handles all types of exceptions thrown during the application's execution.

One of the most useful features of Laravel is the ability to create custom error pages to effectively handle errors and provide users with a better user experience.

To create a custom error page in Laravel, you can use the `render` method in the `App\Exceptions\Handler` file, which allows you to define how to handle a particular type of exception. For example, to handle a 404

"Not Found" error, you can add the following code to the `render` method:

```php
public function render($request, Exception $exception)

{

    if ($exception instanceof ModelNotFoundException) {

        return response()->view('errors.404', [], 404);

    }


    return parent::render($request, $exception);

}
```

In this way, when a `ModelNotFoundException` exception is raised, Laravel will return the `errors.404` view with a status code of 404 (Not Found) to indicate that the page was not found.

To create a custom error page, you can create a `404.blade.php` file in the `resources/views/errors` folder, which will contain the customized error message for the 404 error.

```html
<!DOCTYPE html>

<html>

<head>

    <title>Errore 404 - Pagina non trovata</title>

</head>

<body>

    <h1>Errore 404 - Pagina non trovata</h1>

    <p>La pagina che stai cercando non è disponibile al momento. Ti preghiamo di controllare l'URL o di tornare alla homepage.</p>

</body>

</html>
```

```

In this way, when a user tries to access a non-existent page, the customized error page with the message defined in the `404.blade.php` file will be displayed.

Error handling in Laravel is essential to provide users with an optimal user experience, and creating customized error pages allows errors to be managed effectively and provides users with clear and informative feedback in case of issues.
```

13. Using logs for debugging Exception handling in Laravel

To use logs for debugging in Laravel, you need to correctly configure the `.env` file to specify the desired logging level. You can set the logging level to `debug`, `info`, `notice`, `warning`, `error`, `critical`, `alert`, or `emergency`, depending on the level of detail needed.

Once the desired logging level is configured, you can use Laravel's `Log` function to record debug messages within your code. For example, to log a debug message within a controller, you can use the following code:

```php
use Illuminate\Support\Facades\Log;


public function index()
{
```

```
    Log::debug('This is a debug message');


    // Controller code

}
```


Log messages will be recorded in the file specified in the `config/logging.php` file, usually `storage/logs/laravel.log`. This file can be viewed to check the debug messages recorded during the application's execution.

Additionally, Laravel provides various features to handle exceptions within applications. You can use the `try-catch` block to handle exceptions and provide specific behavior in case of an error. For example:


```php
try {
```

```
    // Code that might throw an exception
} catch (Exception $e) {

    Log::error($e->getMessage());


    // Specific behavior in case of an error

}
```

Furthermore, you can use the `report` function in the `app\Exceptions\Handler.php` file to log unhandled exceptions and notify developers in case of a critical error. This way, you can track errors and quickly resolve them during the application's development.

By using logs for debugging and properly handling exceptions in Laravel, you can easily identify and resolve any issues within the application to ensure optimal functionality and a better user experience.

14. Using External Services in Laravel
Using External APIs in Laravel

Thanks to its flexibility and scalability, it is easy to use external services to enhance the functionality of Laravel applications.

To use external services in Laravel, you need to configure the integration with the API provided by the external service. This usually involves obtaining an access token or the necessary API keys to authenticate and access the data. Once you have obtained this information, you can use libraries like Guzzle to make HTTP requests to the external API and retrieve the desired data.

For example, if you want to integrate an external payment service into your Laravel application, you can use the APIs provided by the payment service to conduct online transactions. Through the integration of these APIs, you can securely and efficiently manage payment transactions directly within the Laravel application.

Another area where using external APIs in Laravel can be advantageous is in integrating with third-party services like Google Maps, Facebook, Twitter, etc. These services offer a wide range of functionalities that can be easily integrated into your Laravel applications to enhance the user experience.

Using external services and APIs in Laravel allows you to expand the functionality of your applications, improve the user experience, and provide new business opportunities. Thanks to its flexibility and built-in support for integrating with external services, Laravel remains one of the best frameworks for developing modern and scalable web applications.

In Laravel, you can use external services and APIs to integrate external functionalities into your projects. There are various libraries and packages available that simplify interaction with external services and APIs.

To get started, you need to install the Guzzle HTTP Client package, which is one of the most popular libraries for making HTTP requests in PHP. To install Guzzle, run the command:

```
composer require guzzlehttp/guzzle
```

Once Guzzle is installed, you can use it to make requests to external services and APIs. For example, if you wanted to make a GET request to the GitHub API to retrieve information about a repository, you could do so like this:

```php
```

```php
use GuzzleHttp\Client;

$client = new Client();
$response = $client->request('GET', 'https://api.github.com/repos/laravel/laravel');

$repository = json_decode($response->getBody());

echo $repository->name; // Output: Laravel
echo $repository->description; // Output: A PHP framework for web artisans
```

In this example, we are using Guzzle to make a GET request to the GitHub API to get information about the Laravel repository. The `request()` method of Guzzle accepts the HTTP method to use (GET, POST, etc.) and the URL of the API to make the request to. Once we receive the response, we decode it as JSON and access the repository information using object syntax.

If the API requires authentication, you can pass the credentials as options in the request. For example, if you wanted to authenticate with the GitHub API, you could do something like this:

```php
$response = $client->request('GET', 'https://api.github.com/user', [

    'auth' => ['username', 'password']

]);
```

This way, you can use external services and APIs in Laravel to add advanced functionality to your projects. Make sure to read the documentation of the API you are using to learn about the available methods and the information required to make correct requests.

15. Integration with cloud services such as AWS or Google Cloud using external packages via Composer in Laravel

Integration with cloud services such as AWS or Google Cloud is essential to enhance the capabilities of a web application developed with Laravel. These services offer a wide range of functionalities such as storage, computing, data management, and much more, which can be used to optimize performance and improve the efficiency of the application.

To integrate these cloud services into a Laravel project, you can use the APIs provided by AWS and Google Cloud, which allow you to access all the functionalities offered by these services in a simple and intuitive way. For example, you can use the AWS API to upload files to S3 or perform computing operations on EC2, or use the Google Cloud API to manage data on Firestore or perform analysis on BigQuery.

Additionally, you can use external packages via Composer to facilitate integration with these cloud services. Composer is a dependency manager for PHP that allows you to easily install and manage external packages within a Laravel project. There are numerous packages available on Packagist that offer specific functionalities for integrating with cloud services like AWS and Google Cloud, such as "aws/aws-sdk-php" for interacting with the AWS API or "google/cloud-storage" for interacting with Google Cloud Storage.

By using Composer to manage these external packages, you can quickly integrate the functionalities offered by cloud services into your Laravel projects without having to write code from scratch. This allows you to save time and resources and focus more on developing the application, leveraging the capabilities offered by the most advanced cloud services on the market.

Integrating cloud services such as AWS or Google Cloud is a common practice in creating modern and scalable applications. In this context, Laravel, a widely used PHP framework for web application development, offers excellent compatibility with both cloud services and allows you to efficiently and simply leverage their functionalities.

Using cloud services like AWS or Google Cloud with Laravel is relatively simple thanks to the libraries and external packages available for integration. In particular, Composer, Laravel's dependency manager, allows you to easily install external packages and third-party libraries to extend the framework's functionalities and integrate with cloud services.

To integrate a cloud service like AWS with Laravel, for example, you can use the package "aws/aws-sdk-php", which provides a PHP interface to interact with AWS cloud services. To install the package, simply run the command:

```bash
composer require aws/aws-sdk-php
```

Once the package is installed, you can use it within your Laravel applications to access AWS services, such as uploading files to Amazon S3 or using Amazon DynamoDB for data storage.

Here is a simple example of how to use the AWS SDK package with Laravel to upload a file to Amazon S3:

```php
use Aws\S3\S3Client;

$s3 = new S3Client([
    'version' => 'latest',
    'region'  => 'us-west-2',
    'credentials' => [
        'key'    => 'your-access-key',
        'secret' => 'your-secret-key',
    ],
]);

$result = $s3->putObject([
    'Bucket' => 'your-bucket-name',
    'Key'    => 'path/to/your/file.txt',
    'Body'   => 'Hello, World!',
]);
```

```
echo 'File uploaded to Amazon S3!';
```
```

In this example, an S3Client object is instantiated using the access credentials provided by AWS, and a text file is uploaded to the specified S3 bucket.

Similarly, you can integrate cloud services like Google Cloud with Laravel using the respective libraries and external packages available on Composer.

In conclusion, integrating cloud services like AWS or Google Cloud with Laravel through Composer allows you to enhance your web applications with advanced and scalable features, providing developers with the flexibility to leverage the capabilities of cloud services in creating modern and efficient applications.
```

16.Performance optimization in Laravel Using cache to improve performance

Performance optimizations are a fundamental aspect in the development of any web application, and Laravel offers a variety of tools to improve the performance of your code. One of the most powerful techniques for optimizing performance in Laravel is using cache.

Cache is a mechanism that temporarily stores data so that it can be accessed more quickly in the future. This can be particularly useful to avoid running costly database queries or calculating complex data every time they are requested.

In Laravel, you can use cache to store the results of database queries, results from external API calls, or any other data that may be used multiple times. To configure cache in Laravel, you can use drivers like Redis,

Memcached, or files to efficiently store the data.

To use cache in Laravel, you can use the `cache()` method available throughout the framework. For example, to store the result of a database query in cache, you can use the following code:

```
$users = cache()->remember('users', 60, function () {

    return DB::table('users')->get();

});
```

In this case, the result of the database query is stored in cache with the key 'users' for 60 minutes. If the data is requested again within 60 minutes, Laravel will return the data stored in cache instead of running the database query again.

Using cache in Laravel can significantly improve the performance of web applications, reducing the load on the database and decreasing response times for requests. However, it is important to carefully consider which data to store in cache and for how long, to avoid storing outdated or unnecessary data. By judiciously using cache, you can significantly improve the performance of a Laravel application and provide users with a faster and more responsive experience.

Using cache in Laravel is very simple and can be done using different methodologies like file cache, database cache, memory cache, and Redis cache. In this article, we will focus on using file cache and memory cache to improve the performance of a Laravel application.

To use file cache in Laravel, you simply need to configure the cache driver in the `config/cache.php` file and specify the location to store the cache data. For example, you can set the cache driver to `file` and specify the folder path to store the cache files. Once configured correctly, you can use the Laravel `Cache` class to store and retrieve data from the cache.

For example, suppose you want to store the result of a costly database query for a certain period of time using file cache. You can do something like this in your controller:

```
```

use Illuminate\Support\Facades\Cache;

use App\Models\Article;

public function index()

{

    $articles = Cache::remember('articles', 60, function () {
```
```

```
    return Article::all();

});


    return view('articles.index',
compact('articles'));

}
```

In this example, the `remember` method of the `Cache` class will store the result of the `Article::all()` query in the cache for 60 seconds using the key `'articles'`. If the key is present in the cache, the stored value will be returned instead of running the expensive query again.

Alternatively, you can use the memory cache to store data in RAM to further improve application performance. In this case, you can configure the cache driver in the `config/cache.php` file and use Laravel's `Cache` class to store and retrieve data from the memory cache.

For example, suppose we want to store the result of an expensive query in the database for a certain period of time using the memory cache. We can do something like this in our controller:

```
use Illuminate\Support\Facades\Cache;

use App\Models\Article;


public function index()
{
    $articles = Cache::remember('articles', 60,
```

```
function () {

    return Article::all();

});


  return view('articles.index',
compact('articles'));

}
```

In this case as well, the `remember` method of the `Cache` class will store the result of the `Article::all()` query in the memory cache for 60 seconds using the key `'articles'`. If the key is present in the cache, the stored value will be returned instead of running the expensive query again.

Using file cache or memory cache in Laravel can significantly improve application performance by reducing page load times and optimizing expensive operations. It is important to evaluate which type of cache is more suitable for your needs and properly configure the cache driver in the `config/cache.php` file to achieve the best possible performance.

17. SQL query optimization with Eloquent Using codebase and job queues for asynchronous operations

Optimizing SQL queries with Eloquent is crucial to ensure optimal performance in our database. Eloquent is an Object-Relational Mapping (ORM) that allows us to interact with the database using objects instead of writing SQL queries manually.

To optimize queries with Eloquent, we can follow various approaches. Firstly, it is important to use eager loading features to load related data in advance and avoid additional queries. For example, we can use the `with()` method to load relation data in a single query instead of making a separate query for each relation.

Another technique to optimize queries is to use indexes on the most commonly used columns in queries. Indexes speed up searches in the database by providing faster access to data. We can create indexes directly on desired columns using Laravel migrations.

As for asynchronous operations, we can use codebases and job queues to execute operations in the background and improve our system's performance. Codebases allow us to enqueue jobs and run them asynchronously, avoiding blocking the main thread of our server.

Using job queues allows us to efficiently handle long and heavy operations, ensuring that our server remains responsive and fast. We can create custom jobs to perform specific operations in the background and monitor progress using Laravel Horizon. Optimizing SQL queries with Eloquent and using codebases and job queues for asynchronous operations are fundamental practices to enhance our system's performance and provide optimal user experience. These techniques enable efficient data management in our database and greater scalability of our system.

Here is an example of how to use job queues with Eloquent in Laravel:

```php
use Illuminate\Support\Facades\Queue;


Queue::push(function () {

    // Operations to be performed asynchronously

});
```

In this way, the anonymous function will be executed in a work queue managed by Laravel, allowing the application to continue responding to requests efficiently. Optimizing SQL queries with Eloquent and using codebases and job queues are fundamental practices to ensure optimal performance of web applications. With these tools, it is possible to efficiently manage complex operations and enhance user experience.

18. Deployment of a Laravel Application Using tools like Docker to manage deployment Best practices for deploying a Laravel application

The deployment of a Laravel application is a fundamental process to ensure that the software can run efficiently and reliably. Using tools like Docker to manage deployment can greatly simplify the process, allowing you to easily create virtualized environments that replicate the production environment.

To start, it is important to create a development environment where you can test and optimize the Laravel application before proceeding with deployment. This environment should include a copy of the application, a test database, and potentially other services like a web server and cache.

Once the application has been tested and is

ready for deployment, it is essential to follow best practices to ensure a smooth and problem-free process. Some helpful tips include:

- Use a version control system like Git to manage the application's source code and ensure traceability of changes.

- Automate the deployment process using tools like Jenkins or Travis CI to ensure that the software is released consistently and reliably.

- Use a configuration management system like Ansible or Puppet to efficiently manage production environment configurations.

- Use Docker or similar tools to create containerized images of the application and any services it interacts with.

- Use a monitoring system like Nagios or New Relic to track application performance and identify any deployment issues.

By following these best practices and using tools like Docker to manage deployment, you can ensure that the Laravel application runs efficiently, securely, and scalably.

Best practices for deploying a Laravel application using Docker:

1. **Using Docker to create an isolated environment**: Docker allows you to create lightweight and isolated containers that contain everything the application needs to function correctly, including source code, dependencies, server configurations, and so on. This avoids problems related to differences between development and production environments.

2. **Using Docker Compose to orchestrate containers**: Docker Compose is a tool that allows you to define and manage multi-container Docker applications. It is useful for managing the execution of multiple containers

simultaneously and defining dependencies between them.

3. **Using a .env file to manage environment variables**: Laravel uses a .env file to manage the application's environment variables, such as database credentials, site URL, and other configurations. It is important to keep this file separate from the source code and populate it correctly during the application deployment.

4. **Using a continuous integration/continuous deployment (CI/CD) service**: A CI/CD service like GitHub Actions, Travis CI, or GitLab CI can automate the application deployment process, running automatic tests, generating distributable builds, and deploying the application to the production server securely and reliably.

Example of deploying a Laravel application using Docker:

Let's say we have a Laravel application called "myapp" and we want to manage the deployment using Docker. Here are the main steps we could follow:

1. Create a Dockerfile in the root of the Laravel project:

```Dockerfile
FROM php:7.4-fpm

WORKDIR /var/www/html

COPY . .

RUN apt-get update && apt-get install -y \
```

```
    git \

    curl \

    libpng-dev \

    libonig-dev \

    libxml2-dev \

    zip \

    unzip


RUN docker-php-ext-install pdo_mysql
mbstring exif pcntl bcmath gd


COPY --from=composer:latest
/usr/bin/composer /usr/bin/composer


RUN composer install


RUN cp .env.example .env
```

```
CMD php artisan serve --host=0.0.0.0
--port=8000

```

2. Create a docker-compose.yml file to define the services and dependencies of the application:

```yaml
version: '3'

services:
  app:
    build:
      context: .
      dockerfile: Dockerfile
    ports:
      - "8000:8000"
    environment:
      - APP_ENV=production
      - APP_KEY=base64:gWnBO43=
      - DB_CONNECTION=mysql
```

```
      - DB_HOST=database

      - DB_PORT=3306

      - DB_DATABASE=myapp

      - DB_USERNAME=root

      - DB_PASSWORD=password

    depends_on:

      - database


  database:

    image: mysql:5.7

    environment:

      MYSQL_ROOT_PASSWORD: password

      MYSQL_DATABASE: myapp
```

3. Run the commands to create and start the Docker containers:

```bash
docker-compose up --build
```

This way, we have created an isolated Docker environment that contains everything the Laravel application needs to function properly, and we have defined the necessary environment variables and dependencies for the application to work. This allows us to efficiently manage the deployment of the application and ensure that it runs correctly on the production server.

19. Eloquent: Laravel's Eloquent ORM, Eloquent relationships, one-to-many, many-to-many, and polymorphic relationships in Eloquent, Migration in Laravel Eloquent, and Seeder in Laravel CRUD operations

Eloquent is Laravel's ORM (Object-Relational Mapping) that allows interacting with the database in a simple and intuitive way through the use of models. With Eloquent, CRUD operations (Create, Read, Update, Delete) can be performed without writing SQL queries manually.

Eloquent relationships allow defining connections between different models, enabling efficient data correlations in the database. The main relationships supported by Eloquent include: one-to-many relationships, many-to-many relationships, and polymorphic relationships.

An example of a one-to-many relationship could be between two models "User" and "Post". Each user can have multiple posts, while each post belongs to only one user. To define this relationship in Laravel, the "hasMany" method in the User model and the "belongsTo" method in the Post model can be used.

Example:

```php
// User model
class User extends Model {
    public function posts() {
        return $this->hasMany('App\Post');
    }
}

// Post model
class Post extends Model {
```

```php
    public function user() {

        return $this->belongsTo('App\User');

    }

}
```

To handle many-to-many relationships between models, such as between "User" and "Role", the "belongsToMany" method can be used.

Example:
```php
// User model
class User extends Model {

    public function roles() {

        return $this->belongsToMany('App\Role');

    }
```

```
}


// Role model

class Role extends Model {

    public function users() {

        return $this-
>belongsToMany('App\User');

    }

}
```
```

Polymorphic relationships allow a model to be associated with various other models without the need to duplicate code. For example, a polymorphic relationship can be used to associate a "Comment" model with different other models like "Post" or "Article".


To create the necessary database tables for the models in Laravel, Migration can be used.
```

Migration allows defining the database schema through PHP code instead of writing SQL scaffolding.

Example:

```bash
php artisan make:migration create_users_table
```

To populate the database with sample data, Seeders can be used. Seeders allow inserting predefined data into the database automatically.

Esempio:

```php
php artisan make:seeder UsersTableSeeder
```

The use of Eloquent makes managing relationships between models in Laravel easier and more intuitive, facilitating the development of complex and scalable web applications.

Controller:

```php
namespace App\Http\Controllers;

use App\Models\Post;
use Illuminate\Http\Request;

class PostController extends Controller
```

```php
{
    public function index()
    {
        $posts = Post::all();
        return view('posts.index', compact('posts'));
    }

    public function create()
    {
        return view('posts.create');
    }

    public function store(Request $request)
    {
        $post = new Post();
        $post->title = $request->title;
```

```php
        $post->content = $request->content;

        $post->save();


        return redirect('/posts');
    }


    public function edit(Post $post)
    {
        return view('posts.edit', compact('post'));
    }


    public function update(Request $request,
Post $post)
    {
        $post->title = $request->title;

        $post->content = $request->content;

        $post->save();
```

```
        return redirect('/posts');

    }


    public function destroy(Post $post)

    {

        $post->delete();


        return redirect('/posts');

    }
}
```

Interfaces:

```php
namespace App\Repositories;
```

```php
use App\Models\Post;

interface PostRepositoryInterface
{
    public function all();

    public function create(array $data);

    public function find($id);

    public function update(array $data, Post $post);

    public function delete(Post $post);
}
```

```php
namespace App\Repositories;

use App\Models\Post;

class PostRepository implements PostRepositoryInterface
{
    public function all()
    {
        return Post::all();
    }

    public function create(array $data)
    {
        return Post::create($data);
```

```php
    }

    public function find($id)
    {
        return Post::findOrFail($id);
    }

    public function update(array $data, Post $post)
    {
        $post->update($data);

        return $post;
    }

    public function delete(Post $post)
    {
        $post->delete();
```

```
    }

}
```
```

In this example, the controller manages the CRUD operations of a "Post" model using interfaces and the repository class to separate the business logic from the presentation logic.
```

20.Example: Creating an e-commerce application in Laravel

Creating an e-commerce application in Laravel, here is an example of how you could start:

1. Create a new Laravel project using the composer command:

```bash
composer create-project --prefer-dist
laravel/laravel eshop
```

2. Configure the database in the .env file with the database access information:

```
```

```
DB_CONNECTION=mysql

DB_HOST=127.0.0.1

DB_PORT=3306

DB_DATABASE=eshop

DB_USERNAME=root

DB_PASSWORD=
```

3. Create controllers for managing products and categories:

```bash
php artisan make:controller ProductController

php artisan make:controller CategoryController
```

4. Define routes in the routes/web.php file to

handle user requests:

```php
Route::get('/products', 'ProductController@index');

Route::get('/products/{id}', 'ProductController@show');

Route::get('/categories', 'CategoryController@index');

Route::get('/categories/{id}', 'CategoryController@show');
```

5. Create models for Product and Category using the command:

```bash
php artisan make:model Product

php artisan make:model Category
```

```
```

6. Add relationships between the Product and Category models in the code:

```php
// In the Product model
public function category() {
    return $this->belongsTo(Category::class);
}

// In the Category model
public function products() {
    return $this->hasMany(Product::class);
}
```

7. Implement functions in the controllers to retrieve data from the database and return the appropriate views.

Index

www.ingramcontent.com/pod-product-compliance
Lightning Source LLC
La Vergne TN
LVHW051700050326
832903LV00032B/3917